Rhode Island

By Susan Labella

Subject Consultant
Deb Zepp
Principal
Matunuck Elementary School
Wakefield, Rhode Island

Reading Consultant
Cecilia Minden-Cupp, PhD
Former Director of the Language and Literacy Program
Harvard Graduate School of Education
Cambridge, Massachusetts

Children's Press®
A Division of Scholastic Inc.
New York   Toronto   London   Auckland   Sydney
Mexico City   New Delhi   Hong Kong
Danbury, Connecticut

Designer: Herman Adler Design
Photo Researcher: Caroline Anderson
The photo on the cover shows mansions along the coast in Newport,
Rhode Island.

Library of Congress Cataloging-in-Publication Data

Labella, Susan, 1948–
  Rhode Island / by Susan Labella.
      p. cm. — (Rookie read-about geography)
  Includes index.
  ISBN-10: 0-516-25388-3 (lib. bdg.)   0-531-16787-9 (pbk.)
  ISBN-13: 978-0-516-25388-6 (lib. bdg.)   978-0-531-16787-8 (pbk.)
  1. Rhode Island—Juvenile literature. 2. Rhode Island—Geography—Juvenile
literature. I. Title. II. Series.
  F79.3.L33 2006
  974.5—dc22   2005024568

c ·1
2/08

CHILDREN'S PRESS, and ROOKIE READ-ABOUT®,
and associated logos are trademarks and/or registered trademarks
of Scholastic Library Publishing. SCHOLASTIC and associated logos
are trademarks and/or registered trademarks of Scholastic Inc.

1 2 3 4 5 6 7 8 9 10 R 16 15 14 13 12 11 10 09 08 07

Which state is called
the Ocean State?
It's Rhode Island!

Rhode Island is in the northeastern part of the United States. It is the smallest state. The main part of Rhode Island touches Massachusetts and Connecticut. Several small islands lie to the east of this main area.

Can you find Rhode Island on this map?

CANADA

WASHINGTON

OREGON

IDAHO

MONTANA

NORTH DAKOTA

SOUTH DAKOTA

WYOMING

NEVADA

UTAH

CALIFORNIA

ARIZONA

NEW MEXICO

MINNESOTA

WISCONSIN

MICHIGAN

IOWA

NEBRASKA

COLORADO

KANSAS

ILLINOIS

INDIANA

MISSOURI

OKLAHOMA

ARKANSAS

TEXAS

KENTUCKY

TENNESSEE

MISSISSIPPI

ALABAMA

LOUISIANA

GEORGIA

FLORIDA

NEW HAMPSHIRE

VERMONT

MAINE

MASSACHUSETTS

NEW YORK

RHODE ISLAND

PENNSYLVANIA

CONNECTICUT

NEW JERSEY

OHIO

WEST VIRGINIA

DELAWARE

VIRGINIA

MARYLAND

Washington, D.C.

NORTH CAROLINA

SOUTH CAROLINA

North

West   East

South

ALASKA   CANADA

MEXICO

HAWAII

5

Rhode Island has miles of beach along the Atlantic Ocean. These beaches are perfect for swimming and fishing!

Narragansett (nare-uh-GAN-sett) Bay is in the eastern part of Rhode Island.

Seals live in Narragansett Bay from October to April every year. They like spending winter in the bay's warm waters.

A lighthouse on Block Island

Block Island is about
10 miles (16 kilometers)
south of the main part
of Rhode Island. Visitors
must take a special boat
called a ferry to get to
Block Island.

Block Island has sailboat
races, nature trails, and
lighthouses. Lighthouses
are used to guide ships
safely to shore.

Providence is the capital of Rhode Island. It is also the largest city in Rhode Island.

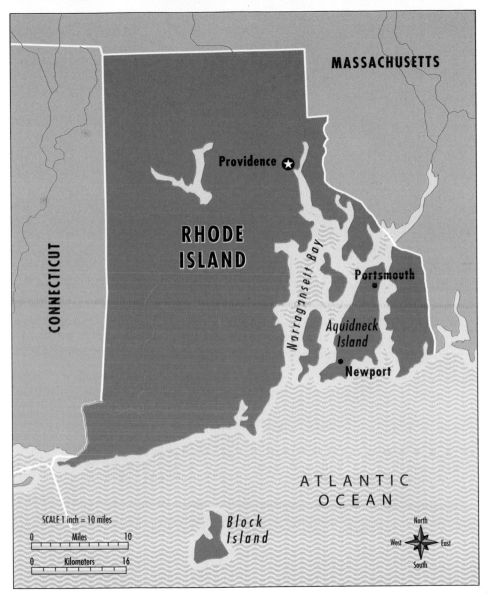

MASSACHUSETTS

Providence ☆

RHODE
ISLAND

CONNECTICUT

Narragansett Bay

Portsmouth

Aquidneck
Island

Newport

ATLANTIC
OCEAN

SCALE 1 inch = 10 miles

0   Miles   10

0   Kilometers   16

Block
Island

North
West ✦ East
South

13

Roger Williams Park is in Providence. People can go on pony rides or visit the zoo. The zoo is home to more than nine hundred animals!

Newport is another city in Rhode Island. It is on Aquidneck (ah-KWID-nek) Island in Narragansett Bay. Newport is famous for its many beautiful, old homes, called mansions.

One of Newport's elegant mansions

This Rhode Island factory worker makes copper products.
Copper is a type of metal.

18

Many people live and work in Rhode Island. Some workers make metal tools in Rhode Island's factories.

Others have jobs in hospitals or work for the government.

Some people in Rhode Island build boats and ships. Others work as fishers.

A group of Rhode Island fishers

Many different trees and flowers grow in Rhode Island. The state tree is the red maple.

A red maple

Rhode Island's state
flower is the violet.

There is a special garden in the town of Portsmouth. All of the bushes in this garden are shaped like animals!

Water birds called great egrets live in Rhode Island.

Many real animals also live in Rhode Island. Water birds build nests near the shore.

Squirrels, foxes, and deer
live in the forests.

Rhode Island is filled
with things to see and do!

What will you do first
when you visit?

Words You Know

Atlantic Ocean

fox

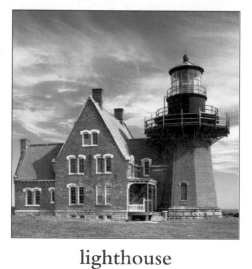

lighthouse

mansions

red maple

scals

violet

zoo

31

Index

About the Author

Susan Labella is a former teacher and editor. She is currently a freelance writer and has written other books in the Rookie Read-About® Geography series.

Photo Credits

Photographs © 2007: Alamy Images/B. Mete Uz: 26; Corbis Images: 22, 31 top left (F. Damm/zefa), 17, 30 bottom right (Wolfgang Kaehler), cover, 25 (Bob Krist), 14, 31 bottom right (Bob Rowan/Progressive Image), 21 (Onne van der Wal); Dembinsky Photo Assoc./Carl R. Sams II: 27, 30 top right; Paul Rezendes: 3, 10, 30 top left, 30 bottom left; Superstock, Inc.: 29 (age fotostock), 18 (David Forbert); The Image Works/Peter Hvizdak: 6, 9, 31 top right; Visuals Unlimited/David Sieren: 23, 31 bottom left.

Maps by Bob Italiano